Chapter 1 – Introduction

So, you have or are thinking about signing up for an Ironman Triathlon. You are inspired and enthusiastic about competing against the 114.6-mile course which includes a 2.4-mile swim, 112 miles on a bike followed by a 26.2 miles' marathon run. Before completing an Ironman, I used to think of the athletes as 'superhuman freaks'; that was until I completed one myself.

Let me give you a bit of background on myself and how I ended up signing up for my first Ironman Triathlon without being able to swim more than a couple of lengths of a 25-meter pool or even owning a road bike. I have played team sports all my playing at a full-time professional standard for a while. Once dropping down to semi-professional I first encountered the problems associated with fitting training in around a 9-5 Monday to Saturday job...ultimately the job won and I decided to retire at the age of 26. Once the training stopped and I had more free weekends to socialise my weight ballooned from 14st 7lb (203lbs) to 16st 7lb (231lbs) and beyond! At this point after a holiday to Mexico I decided enough was enough and I needed to sort myself and my lifestyle out.

At this point I took up running as a way to lose the weight (which I did) and quickly found my way into exploring the world of triathlon as the variety of training appealed to me as it avoided the mundane. I quickly signed up for the Ironman UK 2012 as I found out that a friend was training for an Ironman Triathlon. What I hadn't realised was that he was in training during 2012 for the IMUK 2013! Long story short, I found myself running down the 'golden carpet' with a voice proclaiming "YOU ARE AN IRONMAN" a few months later and have never looked back.

My aim with this booklet is to give guidance and hopefully confidence in the fact that us 'normal people' (i.e. not stick thin gazelles) can complete an ironman triathlon too!

Chapter 2 - Preparation

OK, so you've decided you are going to undertake an Ironman. You have watched a couple of motivational videos on YouTube, you have logged onto the site, entered your details, paid your fee, told everybody you know about it on Facebook and Twitter and have undertaken a sponsorship drive for the charity of your choice. Life is good and you feel good about it.

At some point the enormity of what you have signed up for will hit you. It could be when you wake up in the middle of the night for a pee, when you start to read an article on the number of hours the Pro's put into training on a weekly basis or when you attempt your first swim in the pool and struggle to complete ten lengths.

Do not panic! As daunting as it feels at this moment in time this is an achievable life changing challenge which will push you to your limits. If you put the right training and preparation in you will stand (or float) at the start line knowing that this is going to be one of the most amazing days of your life.

The following Chapters will take you through planning, executing and recovering in the weeks and months up to your Ironman event. The Chapters are aimed to be succinct and to the point in topics which are notoriously full of differing opinions and supporting scientific proof. The Chapters are based upon my findings during my journey to completing the four Ironman events that I have to date with a lot of reading, picking peoples brains and trial and error.

Completing an Ironman is tough and should be given the respect that it deserves in the training and preparation that is made but caution should be taken in not giving the event too much respect in that it becomes crippling in your pursuit of glory.

Chapter 3 – Training Plan

There are a million and one training plans out there and I have experimented with most of them at some point in the last few years. One common denominator of any training plan hinges around the phases of the plans being Preparation, Base, Build, Peak and Race with differing terminology used within different plans.

For me the key to your training plan is the length of each of the above phases depending upon whether you are "the Hare or the Tortoise" i.e. are you built for speed and shorter sharper exertions or are you more adapted to longer slower types of exercises.

Once you have ascertained the above it is time to work backwards from your Ironman Race Day to when you plan on starting your training plan (at least 13 weeks) following the below:

Date	Phase	
IM-13 Weeks	Preparation	Used primarily to prep you for the next couple of months. Use this time to ensure you have all your gear (covered later) and assess how you can best fit in your training sessions into which days of the week.
IM-10 Weeks	Base	This phase is based on giving your body the required base fitness it will need to Swim, Cycle and Run with maximum efficiency focusing on skills, drills and strength building. If you are a 'Hare' and have longer than 13 weeks this is the phase to extend.
IM-6 Weeks	Build	This phase is more focused with the addition of power and speed during the week in addition to your ongoing weekly endurance sessions at the weekend. If you are the 'Tortoise' and have longer than 13 weeks this is the Phase to Extend.
IM-2 Weeks	Peak (or Taper)	All of your 'money in the bank' sessions are completed before you enter this phase. Give yourself a pat on the back and have confidence that you have put the training in to complete the IM. This phase is a recovery, rest and maintenance phase. The aim here is to ensure that you enter Race Week fully recovered and energised.

Chapter 4 – Training Zones

Training Zones are one of the most useful parameters for an IM athlete both during training and racing as the intensity level required during a session or race is important to ensure that correct pacing and effort is exerted to achieve the required outcome on the day.

There are various ways of monitoring your training zone whilst exercising; Power, Heart Rate (HR) and Rated Perceived Exertion (RPE) to name a few. For the basis of this training plan we will concentrate on the simplest (and most cost effective) methods for each of the disciplines.

Zone	Swim	Bike	Run
Drills	Workout includes lots of drills and no concern for the pace clock. Your RPE is in Zone 1.	Workout is one that is done with your heart rate mostly in training Zones 1 and 2. After a good warm up, include four to eight x30-second accelerations with 1.5- to 2.5-minute easy recoveries. Acceleration means gently building your speed, not all-out sprints.	
Z1	The entire workout is done with your heart rate or RPE in Zone 1.		
	Work on technique with lots of drills or an easy workout using various strokes.	It's best to do this work-out on a flat course.	Best done on a flat course, and ideally on a soft surface like grass or a dirt trail.
Z2	Because there are so many options for pool intervals, use the RPE and the clock to determine your pace.	During bike and run workouts, keep your heart rate in Zones 1 and 2. As you gain fitness, you can spend more time in Zone 2. It is not your goal to see how much time you can spend in Zone 2. A rolling course is ideal.	
Z3	The workout is done in Zones 1 to 3 for all three sports. As you gain fitness, you can spend more time in Zone 3. Keep in mind, though, that it is not your goal to see how much time you can spend in Zone 3.		
	In the pool, use the RPE and your goal race pace to determine your training pace.	A rolling to moderately hilly course for the bike or run is fine. (Hint: try to shy away from extremely hilly Ironman courses for your first event!)	

There are many ways of calculating you Heart Rate Zones but I have found that there isn't much variance between them. I have found the Maffeton (aka Mark Allens preferred) method the best:

Zone	RPE	Heart Rate
1 – Recovery	Gentile Breathing. You can maintain a conversation.	90% of Lactate Threshold =(180 minus age)*0.9
2 – Aerobic	Heavier breathing but you feel you can maintain the pace all day.	100% of Lactate Threshold =(180 minus age)*1
3 – Anaerobic	Difficult to speak. Down to one word sentences.	110% of Lactate Threshold =(180 minus age)*1.1

Chapter 5 – Swimming

The swim tends to be the most feared of the three sports of triathlon and in many cases, is the main reason why many people do not take up the sport in the first place. It is surprising how many people you hear say 'I could do an IM if it wasn't for the Swim'.

Whatever your level, from complete beginner to advanced, the single biggest investment that you can make to ensure you make the 2:20 cut-off time for the swim is to employ the use of a local Swim Coach, ideally a Triathlon Swim Coach as there are subtle but important factors to consider and changes in stroke technique in the world of triathlon and Ironman Open Water Swimming.

Phase	Weekly Sessions	Volume
Preparation	Gradually get into training and a focused routine of exercise. Find a Swim Coach.	2 sessions per week
Base	Short sessions concentrating on skills development using the Swim Coach you found during your Preparation Phase.	2 sessions per week
Build	Continue Coached Swim Sessions with additional long swim per week working up to 4,000m in final Build Week.	2-3 sessions per week NB- open water sessions to be undertaken (minimum 3 in the phase)
Peak	Use two swim sessions during the week as 'active recovery'.	2 sessions per week

Chapter 6 – Cycling

The Bike section of the IM is the longest in proportion by a long way being over 50% of your total IM time. You have up to 10:30 after the start to complete the Bike Section (i.e. 10:30 minus the time it took you to complete the Swim). In other words, you have plenty of time to complete this section and the biggest mistake of athletes undertaking their first IM is to go too fast on the bike and completely fall to pieces on the Marathon run.

There is much debate to be had on whether you should go for a Tri Bike or a Road Bike to compete in your first IM. I have had friends complete the Bike Section in sub-6 hours on a Road Bike, I prefer to use a Road Bike with Tri-Bars fitted and all the Pro's use Tri Bikes pretty much exclusively. We will not be getting into this debate here; the only thing that I will say on the matter is to make sure you are comfortable on the bike and make sure have spent a lot of time in your most Aero Position before Race Day. A Bike Fitting is an essential undertaking to ensure this is the case.

Phase	Weekly Sessions	Volume
Preparation	Gradually get into training and a focused routine of exercise. Buy a bike and/or get a bike fitting.	2 sessions per week
Base	Aim to improve endurance, strength and skills gradually lengthening the workout durations.	2 session per week
Build	Work up to a 6 hours long ride in final week of Build. Work on position and pedaling skills and refine your nutrition plan	4 sessions per week
Peak	Tapering workouts to allow for rest whilst maintaining workout intensity to stay sharp.	Short brick every 3 days' emphasis on bike to run (maintain race pace)

Chapter 7 – Running

The Marathon Run is the final section of the IM and in most people's opinion the most difficult. In all honesty when competing in your first IM event with finishing as your only goal you can enjoy the run knowing that you are almost certainly ensured in the fact of hearing those fateful words "YOU ARE AN IRONMAN!" as even if you use all the 10:30 available to you to reach T2 you still have 6:30 to complete the marathon.

The Run requires the least amount of 'gear' of the 3 disciplines in that you only really need a pair of trainers and off you go. It is a good idea, but not essential, to go to a proper triathlon or running shop which will assess you running style and gait and match you to the most appropriate running shoes. Remember that comfort is paramount here.

Phase	Weekly Sessions	Volume
Preparation	Gradually get into training and focused routine of exercise. Buy running shoes after having a gait assessment.	1 session per week
Base	Aim to improve endurance, strength and skills gradually lengthening the workout durations.	2 sessions per week
Build	1 long run p/w no longer than 3 hours - zone 2 whilst refining nutrition plan. 20-30 min runs after every bike ride.	1 long run Brick after every Ride
Peak	Tapering workouts to allow for rest whilst maintaining workout intensity to stay sharp.	Short brick every 3 days emphasis on bike to run (maintain race pace)

Chapter 8 – Gym Work

Gym work is probably the most neglected area of training by Endurance Athletes, especially Ironman Triathletes due to the already demanding training regime required to ensure completion of the event. However, gym work is one of the one the most important elements when training for an IM not only to increase strength but to also to prevent injuries which could have a catastrophic impact on your training. Back in the 80's Ironman legend Dave Scott even when completing 35,000 meters of swimming, 400 miles of cycling and 70 miles of running per week ensured that he also completed three heavy gym sessions into his weekly routine.

A big reason gym work is neglected is the perception that the extra muscle gained is bad for an endurance sport like triathlon. Which can be true if the muscle has developed using single-joint, bodybuilder-style training. Instead a program that quickly adds incredibly functional muscle and athleticism has proven in studies to improve triathlon performance in all disciplines.

The easiest way to seek out such training sessions is to join-in with a couple of exercise classes at your local gym or health center. Classes like Body Pump and Body Combat mixed with a weekly session of Pilates will aide in maintaining and improving functional strength and warning off unwanted injuries whilst out training.

Chapter 9 – Nutrition

Triathletes are obsessed with nutrition. Calories, carbohydrates, electrolytes, protein, you name it and triathletes obsess over it. Visit any local triathlon club and the discussions are dominated with talk about the latest protein flapjack or beetroot juice supplement. Other than bodybuilders this puts beginner triathletes in a unique position where a mass of information can easily confuse in an area that can be easily simplified.

All current research and evidence, either through testimonials or my own experiences of the last couple of years have lead me down the path of a 'natural' diet. I will not be recommending Paleo as I do not like the whole approach of dictating what you can or cannot eat based upon what was available to our ancestors. It just doesn't feel right to me! I will however, be recommending reducing your carbohydrate intake in-between training. This will mean that a typical day will look something like this:

Breakfast:	**4-5 egg omelette on wholemeal toast**
Lunch:	Meat (chicken, beef, ham etc) with salad / vegetables and some sort of legumes (lentils, black eyed peas etc.).
Dinner:	"Meat and two veg", optionally brown rice, quinoa, sweet potato etc.
Snacks:	Protein shakes / protein bars, smoothies (reduce/remove intake of fruit if trying to lose weight)

One thing that needs additional concentrating on is water intake and ensuring that you initially take in 2 litres per day outside of the amount you drink during training. Pre, during and post training ensure that your pre-meal will align with the intensity of the upcoming session (i.e. slightly higher on the carbs if high intensity to ensure quality of the session). Experiment with a 24-hour day-off from the diet to keep yourself sane and allow you a couple of beers/vinos on the weekend. However, if you are not continuing to lose weight after a couple of weeks abandon this approach until you get to your goal weight.

Chapter 10 – Fueling

During a session lasting less than 90 minutes' drink nothing but water. When working-out for longer than 90 mins retain a calorie intake of 4kcal/kg bodyweight/hour be it from Gels, Bars, Isotonic Drinks, Food or a combination of each. After the session have a protein shake with a 3:1 protein to carbs ratio to ensure you are on the path to recovery as soon as possible. Continue in this recovery mode for as long as the session itself lasted before reverting to your 'natural' diet as described in Chapter 9.

Don't fall into the trap that thinking that this is just a swim, a ride and a run. Remember you start off with a 2.4-mile (3.8km) open water swim, then warm those legs up with a 112 miles (180km) cycle and then you need to run a marathon all 26.2 miles (42k) of it.
Fueling is one of the four golden aspects of Ironman – other than Pacing, Heart Rate and Cadence, getting your Fueling right will help to ensure a good race day. Ensuring a good balance between the carbs and protein, along with sufficient electrolyte intake, is the constant nutrition juggle that will have a major impact on both your ability to train and more importantly your ability to recover and train again and again. "Practice, practice, practice" is the nutrition mantra.

Make sure you practice your fueling; Section 12 will cover a detailed breakdown based on fueling during race day and this should be no different to what you do on your 90+ minute training days.

Chapter 11 – Rest

During tough sessions muscle fibers tear producing calcium leakage which makes your body send white blood cells and fluid to the damaged area to start the healing process. You can't throw in another workout until the inflammatory process has taken place and gone away.

Your body has a finite storage of fuel (carbs for example) and you need to give it the opportunity to refill these or you are will be sub-par in training due to this lack of recovery.

Also, there is a mental motivational component to consider. You need a break to allow yourself to come back and perform to the best of your ability in your sessions.

There are so many things that rest gives you that a lot of people miss out on. Mark Allen said that "you are better to be 10% undertrained than 1% over trained". It is a discipline in itself.
Use one, some or all of the below markers before undertaking your days training:

Marker	Indicator
1. Resting HR	Elevated morning pulse is from an overworked nervous system, a sign that you are over trained. Use Apps for tracking your heart rate or something like a fitbit.
2. Body Mass	Losing weight (2% in one day) is a sign that you have a loss of hydration and is a warning sign that you may not be recovered.
3. Quality of sleep	Waking up but not needing a big wee, waking up early or not falling to sleep early? You could be just hungry so have a banana dipped in peanut butter and if you are still struggling to sleep it will be probably due to lack of recovery.
4. Performance	Dead legs, not getting faster (if already doing interval training), performance in your session down on the previous day (pace, speed, watts) are ways of your body telling you to take a rest.
5.Oxygen Saturation	96-99% is the banding you are looking for. A Finger Pulse Oximeter & Heart Rate Monitor will allow you to determine this to assess your recovery.
6.DOMS	This is a normal reaction to training (especially following interval training) but if persistent it is a good indicator that you are not recovered and need to rest.
7.Hydration	The colour of your pee is a great and easy way of reviewing your hydration. If you are peeing yellow you are dehydrated and hydration is key to recovery
8.Appetite	Your appetite goes down if you are not fully recovered or not recovering properly.
9.PAMS (Profile Of Mood States)	Score you mood, when this is low and you are anxious etc. it can be indicative of lack of recovery or overreaching in training. Well-being and happiness is a good sign of decent job of recovering.

Chapter 12 – Diet for Recovery

An anti-inflammatory diet includes foods that naturally contain flavonoids and polyphenols. These are dark fruits (e.g. pomegranate), dark leafy green (e.g. bok choy, kale) and cumin, turmeric's and other Indian type spices.

'Night Shades' (potatoes, tomatoes and peppers) are high in alkaloids which can inhibit recovery. However, these pale into insignificance compared to sugars and starches (high carbs, fruit juice, scones, pizza, pasta, and bagels based diets). These are the worst things you can eat to aid recover as they pose natural anti-inflammatory potential.

These should be replaced with less starchy foods and a high fat food diet (e.g. avocado, oily fish). Don't be concerned about your energy levels as you could take white pasta and replace with quinoa, rice pasta or substitute with squash, beans lentils, sweet potato etc. which will still give you fuel, energy and glycogen to burn but are not as inflammatory as wheat based starches.

Recovery Shake; what you are eating during the day is enough to keep your body fueled. If you are eating when you are hungry and eating healthily your body will restore its glycogen stores within 8 hours so if you plan on working out again within this time frame fill up your body stores within 30 minutes, if not just eat your normal diet. This is also true if you are training in a fasted state (i.e. before breakfast) it is applicable to use the "30 minutes window".

Eating before you go to sleep; if you are not trying to lose weight, you will get a bit of a release of growth hormone to aide recovery if you eat before bed. If you do not want to eat but still want the increase growth hormone you can try gamma-Aminobutyric acid (GABA) before bed. Deep sleep also aides repair and recovery during sleep which can be aided by using magnesium.

Chapter 13 - Supplements for Recovery

You want to give the body more of the tools it needs to naturally speed up the recovery process. When you take Ibuprofen, or the like, it stops the body sending white blood cells to the area and shuts down the recovery process. If you treat the area with ice and little bit of heat to get better blood flow to the area gives the body what it needs to speed up the recovery.

Free radicals are produced during exercise which hold back the recovery process and your body needs help after training with anti-oxidants. Combine eating a healthy diet with taking an anti-oxidant that is as full a spectrum of anti-oxidants you can find in a meal replacement.

Calcium leakage occurs during exercise. Magnesium displaces calcium which rapidly alleviating post workout soreness. Oral use of magnesium is good for sleep but spray on magnesium is far superior for post-race / workouts.

Protein powder should be considered as a real food; mix with oatmeal in the morning for example. Protein powder is very good at giving your body what it needs for repair and recovery however most people eat more protein than they actually need. Eat 0.8-1.0g/lb or 1.8-2.2g/kg body weight per day but no more. Most of the rest of what you eat should come from high amounts of fat and a smart amount of carbs injected when appropriate. Total percentage of your daily calorie intake should be 25-30% protein.

During training sessions, it is also a good option to choose gels/liquids that offer Branch Chain Amino Acids (BCAA) in them (e.g. Gu Roctane). BCAA can decrease levels of post workout soreness, help you to recovery faster and go harder in the session. Also, taking amino acids before your workout can stave off the use of amino acids from your muscles during exercise. Eat steamed chicken, yoghurt or take an amino acid powder.

Chapter 14 - Aides to Recovery

Compression Gear allows your body to milk fluid and inflammatory bi-products up out of an area much easier as it pulls blood from the area you have inflammation and shovels it up towards your heart. With 110 Compression Wear you can put ice packs in which compresses the blood vessels a little bit which dilates and increase blood flow and secretes post workout soreness and recovery. Compression Wear is good for increasing recovery but they won't increase performance. However, if you wear them during an Ironman (for example) it will help with your muscles being constantly jarred especially towards the end of a marathon. You won't go any faster but you'll be less sore during the event and the following day.

A massage or foam roller or muscle stick can be used to reduce muscular adhesion after exercising. This allows the muscle to move more freely and to increase blood flow. Compression wear and a foam roller are massive for recovery. If you are getting a massage don't time it right before or right after a tough session or race.

Electro stimulation is also an option which is a component you attach to the muscle with a pad that simulates massage and forces the muscles to contract and get the blood flowing and increase recovery and reduce soreness, especially if you are going to be sitting down pretty quickly after finishing.

Ice baths can help with soreness after a long run or bike. Fill the bath with ice before you set off and jump in for 20 minutes (grit your teeth and stick with it). Most professional sports teams now use ice baths so that alone speaks for itself. Magnesium / Salt baths the day after exercise (not right after) can really help absorb some of the calcium and soreness.

Active recovery is good if it isn't weight bearing and increases blood flow; walking, riding a bike, swimming, golf etc. (Just don't over do it!).

Chapter 15 – The Taper

There are number of contentious opinions on the taper with most ironman triathletes seeming to purposefully take their body to its limits over several months before commencing a 2-3 week race-taper on the belief (or hope) that they will be raring to go when they hit the start line feeling refreshed and fitter then when they started the journey.

In any other sport this approach would be unheard of. There will always be a need to stress the body for it to adapt and improve but the constant fatiguing of the body over months followed by weeks of rest before the big event is counterintuitive.

The approach I apply is similar to that by weightlifters'. Never train more than 2-3 days before a good rest day. If your pace or speed aren't up in the next workout, take another rest day or two. You can still fit in two-a-day training on occasions (especially during the build when you need to fit 7 sessions in plus gym sessions) but the principle is simple: you should get stronger and faster every week (or day), not just hoping to get there after a 3-4 months of hard work and a 3 week tapering period.

Using this approach you will find that you can fit in all of the training required as outlined in Chapter 16 but should feel constantly refreshed and not under pressure to miss a session if feeling tired - make sure you differentiate between being tired and being lazy!! (see the Recovery section in Chapter 11 for benchmarks for rest).

By following the above you should feel ready to go throughout your training sessions without the need to rest-up for a couple of weeks. Therefore, during the 2 weeks taper recovery sessions make sure to up the tempo in spurts during the sessions to keep you feeling sharp.

Chapter 14 – Race Week

Monday – Thursday continue to follow your Taper plan. Friday consists of going to the Ironman Registration Tent and registering which basically involves picking up a 'free' backpack with you race numbers etc. in there. Try and get a 'quick dip' and swim around a much-reduced course to remind yourself of the key places to sight during the swim so that you can run through this visually throughout the remainder of the weekend. Also make an effort to simulate making you way from the water to T1; again, to help visual the process and to make sure there are no surprises on race day. Attend the Race Brief if there is one as it helps to set the stall for the remainder of the weekend and is a good source of motivation.

Saturday; is the lightest day in many senses of the word. After eating all of the food that you want to on the Friday, try to stick to healthier type Carbs, try to eat light snacks throughout the day so that your stomach never feels too full during the day.

The day usually consists of packing your Transitions Bags, which can be one of the most stressful things to do as you are constantly second guessing yourself and packing and un-packing your bags to make sure that you haven't forgotten anything or you have enough nutrition and 'aides' in the bag that you may or may not need on the day.

Once this is done it was a matter of making your way to T1 and T2 and racking your bike and leaving your T1 and T2 bags behind. Then make your way home and chill out. I like to enjoy a glass of red wine the night before which I find helps me to sleep without any side effects the morning of race day. Maybe a good idea to practice this beforehand!

Chapter 15 - Race Day

You should wake up early feeling engerised. You had done a hell of a let of work to make it to the start line. You should Feel confident; today is Game Day!

Make sure to get to the transition in plenty of time making sure to leave it as late as possible before going into the water as you don't want to be in the water too long, however by mindful that you don't want to leave it too late as there are always people streaming into the water as the hooter sounds!

Regardless of where you start in the group you will find yourself in the hustle and bustle of the 'mosh pit' that is the mass start of the swim. When the hooter sounds go for it in the first hundred meters or so to give myself a bit of space. At the start when in the 'mosh pit' the most important thing is to not panic, you have worked too hard to make it this far!!! Once you get into your rhythm take your time and draft wherever possible going with the flow.

T1 should be as expected as you rehearsed on Friday and ran through mentally the rest of the weekend. These are the simple things that make your day so much smoother.

Set off nice and easy on the bike, and continue to do so for the first 40 miles feeling really strong making sure your nutrition is spot on to plan to remember to drink. Once you up the pace after 40 miles you may start to tire and flag on the back end but keep your heart rate down and maintain a steady cadence and look forward to getting off the bike and starting the run.

Congratulate yourself on a job well done at T2 and be confident that even if you have to drag yourself across the finish line you will make it from here. The marathon is a tough drag and is by no means pretty! There will be a massive concentration of the spectators watching the event who make a hell of a lot of noise so soak it in make use of the aid stations which provide a good array of the nutrition that you need, run within yourself and be immensely proud!!!

Chapter 16 – Weekly Plan

Below is a sample weekly plan for each of the training phases identified above. This is on the basis that you work a 9-5 Monday to Friday job with your longer sessions being undertaken during the weekend. You can vary this accordingly and is only for illustrative purposes. Please take cognisance of your recovery and do not get too eat-up about the number of hours you are training. If someone is bragging that they are doing 15, 20 or even 30+ hours a week they are more than likely putting in 'junk miles' which are of little value. Rest up and train well!

Prep	Mon	Tue	Wed	Thu	Fri	Sat	Sun
Swim		S1		S2			
Bike		B1					B2
Run			R1			R2	
Gym			G1		G2		
Base	**Mon**	**Tue**	**Wed**	**Thu**	**Fri**	**Sat**	**Sun**
Swim		S1		S2			
Bike		B1					B2
Run			R1			R2	
Gym			G1		G2		
Build	**Mon**	**Tue**	**Wed**	**Thu**	**Fri**	**Sat**	**Sun**
Swim		S1		S2			S3
Bike		B1	B2		B3		B4
Run		R1	R2		R3	R4	
Gym				G1		G2	
Peak	**Mon**	**Tue**	**Wed**	**Thu**	**Fri**	**Sat**	**Sun**
Swim		S1		S2			
Bike			B1			B2	
Run			R1			R2	
Race Week	**Mon**	**Tue**	**Wed**	**Thu**	**Fri**	**Sat**	**Sun**
Swim	S1		S2			Short easy course familiarisation as required	RACE DAY... ENJOY!!!
Bike		B1		B2			
Run		R1		R2			

Chapter 17 – Example Daily 13 Weeks Ironman Plan

Prep: **Week 1**   **WC**

Monday			
Resting Heart Rate:		Weight:	
Swim	**Bike**	**Run**	**Other**
00:00	00:00	00:00	0:00
-	-	-	
-	-	-	

Tuesday			
Resting Heart Rate:		Weight:	
Swim	**Bike**	**Run**	**Other**
0:00	01:00	0:00	0:00
			-
			-

Wednesday			
Resting Heart Rate:		Weight:	
Swim	**Bike**	**Run**	**Other**
00:00	00:00	00:00	00:00
-		-	-
-		-	-

Thursday			
Resting Heart Rate:		Weight:	
Swim	**Bike**	**Run**	**Other**
00:00	00:00	00:00	00:45
-	-	-	AA - 3*20
-	-	-	-Squats -Lat pull-down -Leg Press -Chest Press -Seated Row -Hamstring Curl -Abominal twist

Friday			
Resting Heart Rate:		Weight:	
Swim	**Bike**	**Run**	**Other**
00:00	01:00	00:00	00:00
-	BE1	-	-
-	Recovery -Steady Zone 1 -Comfortable high cadence -Flat Course	-	-

Saturday			
Resting Heart Rate:		Weight:	
Swim	**Bike**	**Run**	**Other**
00:00	01:00	01:00	00:00
-	BE2	RE2	-
-	Extensive Endurance -Steady Zone 2 -Comfortable high cadence -Rolling Course	Extensive Endurance - Steady Zone 2 - Cadence 90 - Rolling Course	-

Sunday			
Resting Heart Rate:		Weight:	
Swim	**Bike**	**Run**	**Other**
00:00	00:00	00:00	00:00
-		-	-
-		-	-

TOTAL			

SWIM	BIKE	RUN	OTHER
00:00	03:00	01:00	00:45
		TOTAL	04:45

Prep: **Week 2**   **WC**

Monday

Resting Heart Rate:		Weight:	
Swim	**Bike**	**Run**	**Other**
00:00	00:00	00:00	0:00
-	-	-	
-	-	-	

Tuesday

Resting Heart Rate:		Weight:	
Swim	**Bike**	**Run**	**Other**
0:00	01:00	0:00	00:00
			-
			-

Wednesday

Resting Heart Rate:		Weight:	
Swim	**Bike**	**Run**	**Other**
00:00	0:00	00:00	00:00
-		-	-
-		-	-

Thursday

Resting Heart Rate:		Weight:	
Swim	**Bike**	**Run**	**Other**
00:00	00:00	00:00	00:45
-	-	-	AA - 3*20
-	-	-	-Squats -Lat pull-down -Leg Press -Chest Press -Seated Row -Hamstring Curl -Abominal twist

Friday			
Resting Heart Rate:		Weight:	
Swim	**Bike**	**Run**	**Other**
00:00	01:00	00:00	00:00
-	BE1	-	-
-	Recovery -Steady Zone 1 -Comfortable high cadence -Flat Course	-	-

Saturday			
Resting Heart Rate:		Weight:	
Swim	**Bike**	**Run**	**Other**
00:00	01:00	01:00	00:00
-	BE2	RE2	-
-	Extensive Endurance -Steady Zone 2 -Comfortable high cadence -Rolling Course	Extensive Endurance - Steady Zone 2 - Cadence 90 - Rolling Course	-

Sunday			
Resting Heart Rate:		Weight:	
Swim	**Bike**	**Run**	**Other**
00:00	0:00	00:00	00:00
-		-	-
-		-	-

TOTAL			

SWIM	**BIKE**	**RUN**	**OTHER**
00:00	03:00	01:00	00:45
		TOTAL	04:45

Base   **Week 3**   **WC**

Monday			
Resting Heart Rate:		Weight:	
Swim	**Bike**	**Run**	**Other**
00:00	00:00	00:30	00:45
-	-	RE2	SM - 3*6
-	-	Extensive Endurance - Steady Zone 2 - Cadence 90 - Rolling Course	-Squat -Seated Row -Abdominal Twist -Hamstring Curl -Chest Press

Tuesday			
Resting Heart Rate:		Weight:	
Swim	**Bike**	**Run**	**Other**
	01:00	-	00:00
	BM4	-	-
	Crisscross Threshold - W/up to Zone 4 - Build to Zone 5a within 2 mins - Back off to Zone 4 within 2 mins - Continue pattern - Low cadence - Flat Course	-	-

Wednesday			
Resting Heart Rate:		Weight:	
Swim	**Bike**	**Run**	**Other**
01:00	-	01:00	00:00
SS1	-	RF2	-
Open Water Swim	-	Long Hills -Several 6+ min climbs, Zones 1-5a -'Proud Posture' on climb	-

Thursday			
Resting Heart Rate:		Weight:	
Swim	**Bike**	**Run**	**Other**
00:00	00:00	01:00	00:45
-	-	RM3	SM - 3*6
-	-	Hill Cruise Intervals - 6-12 min Intervals uphill - Zone 4-5a - 3 min recovery in Zone 1 - Rolling Course	-Squat -Seated Row -Abdominal Twist -Hamstring Curl -Chest Press

Friday

Resting Heart Rate:		Weight:	
Swim	**Bike**	**Run**	**Other**
01:00	00:00	00:00	00:00
SBM	-	-	-
Swim Benchmark Workout -10 min w/up -6 x 500m w/ 30 secs recovery -Race Pace maintained throughout	-	-	-

Saturday

Resting Heart Rate:		Weight:	
Swim	**Bike**	**Run**	**Other**
00:00	02:00	01:00	00:00
-	CE1	CE1	-
-	Extensive Endurance Brick -Long Steady Ride Zone 1&2 -Long Steady Run Zone 1&2	Extensive Endurance Brick -Long Steady Ride Zone 1&2 -Long Steady Run Zone 1&2	-

Sunday

Resting Heart Rate:		Weight:	
Swim	**Bike**	**Run**	**Other**
00:00	02:30	00:00	00:00
-	BBM	-	-
-	Cycling Benchmark Workout -30 min w/up -2-4 hour Zone 2 -30 coll down -Nutrition as race day	-	-

TOTAL

SWIM	BIKE	RUN	OTHER
02:00	05:30	03:30	01:30
		TOTAL	12:30

Base   **Week 4**   **WC**

Monday			
Resting Heart Rate:		Weight:	
Swim	**Bike**	**Run**	**Other**
00:00	00:00	00:30	00:45
-	-	RE2	SM - 3*6
-	-	Extensive Endurance - Steady Zone 2 - Cadence 90 - Rolling Course	-Squat -Seated Row -Abdominal Twist -Hamstring Curl -Chest Press

Tuesday			
Resting Heart Rate:		Weight:	
Swim	**Bike**	**Run**	**Other**
-	01:00		00:00
-	BM4		-
-	Crisscross Threshold - W/up to Zone 4 - Build to Zone 5a within 2 mins - Back off to Zone 4 within 2 mins - Continue pattern - Low cadence - Flat Course		-

Wednesday			
Resting Heart Rate:		Weight:	
Swim	**Bike**	**Run**	**Other**
01:00	-	01:00	00:00
SS1	-	RF2	-
Open Water	-	Long Hills -Several 6+ min climbs, Zones 1-5a -'Proud Posture' on climb	-

Thursday			
Resting Heart Rate:		Weight:	
Swim	**Bike**	**Run**	**Other**
00:00	00:00	01:00	00:45
-	-	RM3	SM - 3*6
-	-	Hill Cruise Intervals - 6-12 min uphill - Zone 4-5a - 3 min recovery in Zone 1 - Rolling Course	-Squat -Seated Row -Abdominal Twist -Hamstring Curl -Chest Press

Friday			
Resting Heart Rate:		Weight:	
Swim	**Bike**	**Run**	**Other**
00:00	02:00	00:00	00:00
-	BF2	-	-
-	Long Hills -Several 6+ min climbs -Zones 1-5a -Only stand on short steep climbs -Cadence 60+ rpm	-	-

Saturday			
Resting Heart Rate:		Weight:	
Swim	**Bike**	**Run**	**Other**
00:00	02:00	01:00	00:00
-	CE1	CE1	-
-	Extensive Endurance Brick -Long Steady Ride Zone 1&2 -Long Steady Run Zone 1&2	Extensive Endurance Brick -Long Steady Ride Zone 1&2 -Long Steady Run Zone 1&2	-

Sunday			
Resting Heart Rate:		Weight:	
Swim	**Bike**	**Run**	**Other**
00:00	00:00	00:30	00:00
-	-	RE2	-
-	-	Extensive Endurance - Steady Zone 2 - Cadence 90 - Rolling Course	-

TOTAL			

SWIM	**BIKE**	**RUN**	**OTHER**
01:00	05:00	04:00	01:30
		TOTAL	11:30

Base　　　　**Week 5**　　　**WC**

Monday			
Resting Heart Rate:		Weight:	
Swim	**Bike**	**Run**	**Other**
00:00	00:00	00:30	00:45
-	-	RE2	SM - 3*6
-	-	Extensive Endurance - Steady Zone 2 - Cadence 90 - Rolling Course	-Squat -Seated Row -Abdominal Twist -Hamstring Curl -Chest Press

Tuesday			
Resting Heart Rate:		Weight:	
Swim	**Bike**	**Run**	**Other**
-	01:00	-	00:00
-	BM4	-	-
-	Crisscross Threshold - W/up to Zone 4 - Build to Zone 5a within 2 mins - Back off to Zone 4 within 2 mins - Continue pattern - Low cadence - Flat Course	-	-

Wednesday			
Resting Heart Rate:		Weight:	
Swim	**Bike**	**Run**	**Other**
01:00	-	01:00	00:00
SS1	-	RF2	-
Open Water Swim	-	Long Hills -Several 6+ min climbs -Zones 1-5a -'Proud Posture' on climb	-

Thursday			
Resting Heart Rate:		Weight:	
Swim	**Bike**	**Run**	**Other**
00:00	00:00	01:00	00:45
-	-	RM3	SM - 3*6
-	-	Hill Cruise Intervals - 6-12 min Intervals uphill - Zone 4-5a - 3 min recovery in Zone 1 - Rolling Course	-Squat -Seated Row -Abdominal Twist -Hamstring Curl -Chest Press

Friday			
Resting Heart Rate:		Weight:	
Swim	**Bike**	**Run**	**Other**
00:00	02:00	00:00	00:00
-	BF2	-	-
-	Long Hills -Several 6+ min climbs -Zones 1-5a -Only stand on short steep climbs -Cadence 60+ rpm	-	-

Saturday			
Resting Heart Rate:		Weight:	
Swim	**Bike**	**Run**	**Other**
00:00	02:00		00:00
-	CE1		-
-	Extensive Endurance Brick -Long Steady Ride Zone 1&2 -Long Steady Run Zone 1&2		-

Sunday			
Resting Heart Rate:		Weight:	
Swim	**Bike**	**Run**	**Other**
00:00		3:00	00:00
-		RBM	-
-		Running Benchmark Workout -2:30-3hrs Zone 2	-

TOTAL			
SWIM	**BIKE**	**RUN**	**OTHER**
01:00	05:00	05:30	01:30
		TOTAL	13:00

Base **Week 6** **WC**

Monday			
Resting Heart Rate:		Weight:	
Swim	**Bike**	**Run**	**Other**
00:00	00:00	00:00	00:45
-	-	-	SM - 3*6
-	-	-	-Squat -Seated Row -Abdominal Twist -Hamstring Curl -Chest Press

Tuesday			
Resting Heart Rate:		Weight:	
Swim	**Bike**	**Run**	**Other**
	01:00	-	00:00
	BT2	-	-
	Time Trial - 15-30 min w/up - 10k	-	-

Wednesday			
Resting Heart Rate:		Weight:	
Swim	**Bike**	**Run**	**Other**
01:00		00:30	00:00
SS1		RT2	-
Open Water Swim		Time Trial - 1000m	-

Thursday			
Resting Heart Rate:		Weight:	
Swim	**Bike**	**Run**	**Other**
00:00	00:00	00:30	00:45
-	-	RM3	SM - 3*6
-	-	Hill Cruise Intervals - 6-12 min Intervals uphill - Zone 4-5a - 3 min recovery in Zone 1 - Rolling Course	-Squat -Seated Row -Abdominal Twist -Hamstring Curl -Chest Press

Friday			
Resting Heart Rate:		Weight:	
Swim	**Bike**	**Run**	**Other**
00:00	00:30	00:00	00:00
-	BE2	-	-
-	Extensive Endurance -Steady Zone 2 -Comfortable high cadence -Rolling Course	-	-

Saturday			
Resting Heart Rate:		Weight:	
Swim	**Bike**	**Run**	**Other**
00:00	01:00	00:30	00:00
-	CE1	CE1	-
-	Extensive Endurance Brick -Long Steady Ride Zone 1&2 -Long Steady Run Zone 1&2	Extensive Endurance Brick -Long Steady Ride Zone 1&2 -Long Steady Run Zone 1&2	-

Sunday			
Resting Heart Rate:		Weight:	
Swim	**Bike**	**Run**	**Other**
00:00	00:00	00:00	00:00
-	-	-	-
-	-	-	-

TOTAL			
SWIM	**BIKE**	**RUN**	**OTHER**
01:00	02:30	01:30	01:30
		TOTAL	06:30

Build   Week 7   WC

Monday			
Resting Heart Rate:		Weight:	
Swim	**Bike**	**Run**	**Other**
01:00	00:00	00:00	00:00
SBM	-	-	-
Swim Benchmark Workout -10 min w/up -6 x 500m w/ 30 secs recovery -Race Pace maintained throughout	-	-	-

Tuesday			
Resting Heart Rate:		Weight:	
Swim	**Bike**	**Run**	**Other**
00:00	01:00	00:00	00:00
-	BM4	-	-
-	Crisscross Threshold - W/up to Zone 4 - Build to Zone 5a within 2 mins - Back off to Zone 4 within 2 mins - Continue pattern - Low cadence - Flat Course	-	-

Wednesday			
Resting Heart Rate:		Weight:	
Swim	**Bike**	**Run**	**Other**
01:00	00:00	00:30	00:00
SF1	-	RF2	-
Open Water	-	Long Hills -Several 6+ min climbs, Zones 1-5a -'Proud Posture' on climb	-

Thursday			
Resting Heart Rate:		Weight:	
Swim	**Bike**	**Run**	**Other**
00:00	00:00	00:30	00:00
-	-	RM3	-
-	-	Hill Cruise Intervals - 6-12 min Intervals uphill, Zone 4-5a - 3 min recovery in Zone 1, Rolling Course	-

Friday			
Resting Heart Rate:		Weight:	
Swim	**Bike**	**Run**	**Other**
00:00	01:00	00:00	00:00
-	BF2	-	-
-	Long Hills -Several 6+ min climbs -Zones 1-5a -Only stand on short steep climbs -Cadence 60+ rpm	-	-
Saturday			
Resting Heart Rate:		Weight:	
Swim	**Bike**	**Run**	**Other**
00:00	00:00	02:30	00:00
-	-	RBM	-
-	-	Running Benchmark Workout -2:30-3hrs Zone 2	-
Sunday			
Resting Heart Rate:		Weight:	
Swim	**Bike**	**Run**	**Other**
00:00	04:00	00:00	00:00
-	BBM	-	-
-	Cycling Benchmark Workout -30 min w/up -2-4 hour Zone 2 -30 cool down -Nutrition as race day	-	-
TOTAL			
SWIM	**BIKE**	**RUN**	**OTHER**
01:00	06:00	03:30	00:00
		TOTAL	10:30

Build   **Week 8**   **WC**

Monday			
Resting Heart Rate:		Weight:	
Swim	**Bike**	**Run**	**Other**
00:00	00:00	00:00	00:00
-	-	-	-
-	-	-	-

Tuesday			
Resting Heart Rate:		Weight:	
Swim	**Bike**	**Run**	**Other**
00:00	01:00	00:00	00:00
-	BM4	-	-
-	Crisscross Threshold - W/up to Zone 4 - Build to Zone 5a within 2 mins - Back off to Zone 4 within 2 mins - Continue pattern - Low cadence - Flat Course	-	-

Wednesday			
Resting Heart Rate:		Weight:	
Swim	**Bike**	**Run**	**Other**
01:00	00:00	00:30	00:00
SF1	-	RF2	-
Open Water	-	Long Hills -Several 6+ min climbs, Zones 1-5a -'Proud Posture' on climb	-

Thursday			
Resting Heart Rate:		Weight:	
Swim	**Bike**	**Run**	**Other**
00:00	00:00	00:30	00:00
-	-	RM3	-
-	-	Hill Cruise Intervals - 6-12 min Intervals uphill - Zone 4-5a - 3 min recovery in Zone 1 - Rolling Course	-

Friday			
Resting Heart Rate:		Weight:	
Swim	**Bike**	**Run**	**Other**
00:00	01:00	00:00	00:00
-	BF2	-	-
-	Long Hills -Several 6+ min climbs -Zones 1-5a -Only stand on short steep climbs -Cadence 60+ rpm	-	-

Saturday			
Resting Heart Rate:		Weight:	
Swim	**Bike**	**Run**	**Other**
00:00	00:00	02:30	00:00
-	-	RBM	-
-	-	Running Benchmark Workout -2:30-3hrs Zone 2	-

Sunday			
Resting Heart Rate:		Weight:	
Swim	**Bike**	**Run**	**Other**
00:00	04:00	00:00	00:00
-	BE2	-	-
-	Extensive Endurance -Steady Zone 2 -Comfortable high cadence -Rolling Course	-	-

TOTAL			

SWIM	**BIKE**	**RUN**	**OTHER**
01:00	06:00	03:30	00:00
		TOTAL	10:30

Monday			
Resting Heart Rate:		Weight:	
Swim	**Bike**	**Run**	**Other**
	00:00	00:00	00:00
	-	-	-
	-	-	-

Tuesday			
Resting Heart Rate:		Weight:	
Swim	**Bike**	**Run**	**Other**
00:00	01:00	00:00	00:00
-	BM4	-	-
-	Crisscross Threshold - W/up to Zone 4 - Build to Zone 5a within 2 mins - Back off to Zone 4 within 2 mins - Continue pattern - Low cadence - Flat Course	-	-

Wednesday			
Resting Heart Rate:		Weight:	
Swim	**Bike**	**Run**	**Other**
01:00	00:00	00:30	00:00
SF1	-	RF2	-
Open Water	-	Long Hills -Several 6+ min climbs, Zones 1-5a -'Proud Posture' on climb	-

Thursday			
Resting Heart Rate:		Weight:	
Swim	**Bike**	**Run**	**Other**
00:00	00:00	00:30	00:00
-	-	RM3	-
-	-	Hill Cruise Intervals - 6-12 min Intervals uphill - Zone 4-5a - 3 min recovery in Zone 1 - Rolling Course	-

Friday

Resting Heart Rate:		Weight:	
Swim	**Bike**	**Run**	**Other**
00:00	01:00	00:00	00:00
-	BF2	-	-
-	Long Hills -Several 6+ min climbs -Zones 1-5a -Only stand on short steep climbs -Cadence 60+ rpm	-	-

Saturday

Resting Heart Rate:		Weight:	
Swim	**Bike**	**Run**	**Other**
00:00	00:00	00:00	00:00
-	-		-
-	-		-

Sunday

Resting Heart Rate:		Weight:	
Swim	**Bike**	**Run**	**Other**
01:00	04:30	02:00	00:00
BD	BD	BD	-
Big Day -200m w/up -5x400 (10 sec rest) -500m Time Trial -300m c/down **90 min rest**	**Big Day** -30min w/up -8*20min Z3 (10min easy spin) **90 min rest**	**Big Day** -2 hour Z2	-

TOTAL

SWIM	BIKE	RUN	OTHER
02:00	06:30	03:00	00:00
		TOTAL	11:30

Build   **Week 10**   <u>WC</u>

Monday			
Resting Heart Rate:		Weight:	
Swim	**Bike**	**Run**	**Other**
00:00	00:00	00:00	00:00
-	-	-	-
-	-	-	-

Tuesday			
Resting Heart Rate:		Weight:	
Swim	**Bike**	**Run**	**Other**
00:00	01:00	00:00	00:00
-	BT2	-	-
-	Time Trial - 15-30 min w/up - 10k	-	-

Wednesday			
Resting Heart Rate:		Weight:	
Swim	**Bike**	**Run**	**Other**
01:00	00:00	00:30	00:00
SF1	-	RT2	-
Open Water	-	Time Trial - 1000m	-

Thursday			
Resting Heart Rate:		Weight:	
Swim	**Bike**	**Run**	**Other**
00:00	00:00	00:30	00:00
-	-	RM3	-
-	-	Hill Cruise Intervals - 6-12 min Intervals uphill - Zone 4-5a - 3 min recovery in Zone 1 - Rolling Course	-

Friday			
Resting Heart Rate:		Weight:	
Swim	**Bike**	**Run**	**Other**
00:00	01:00	00:00	00:00
-	BF2	-	-
-	Long Hills -Several 6+ min climbs -Zones 1-5a -Only stand on short steep climbs -Cadence 60+ rpm	-	-
Saturday			
Resting Heart Rate:		Weight:	
Swim	**Bike**	**Run**	**Other**
00:00	01:30	01:00	00:00
-	CE1	CE1	-
-	Extensive Endurance Brick -Long Steady Ride Zone 1&2 -Long Steady Run Zone 1&2	Extensive Endurance Brick -Long Steady Ride Zone 1&2 -Long Steady Run Zone 1&2	-
Sunday			
Resting Heart Rate:		Weight:	
Swim	**Bike**	**Run**	**Other**
00:00	00:00	3:00	00:00
-	-	RBM	-
-	-	Running Benchmark Workout -2:30-3hrs Zone 2	-
TOTAL			
SWIM	**BIKE**	**RUN**	**OTHER**
01:00	03:30	05:00	00:00
		TOTAL	09:30

Peak   **Week 11**   **WC**

Monday			
Resting Heart Rate:		Weight:	
Swim	**Bike**	**Run**	**Other**
00:00	00:00	00:00	00:45
-	-	-	SM - 3*6
-	-	-	-Squat -Seated Row -Abdominal Twist -Hamstring Curl -Chest Press

Tuesday			
Resting Heart Rate:		Weight:	
Swim	**Bike**	**Run**	**Other**
	01:00	00:15	
	CM1	CM1	
	Tempo Brick -60-90min Ride w/20k time trial -15-45min at race pace	Tempo Brick -60-90min Ride w/20k time trial -15-45min at race pace	

Wednesday			
Resting Heart Rate:		Weight:	
Swim	**Bike**	**Run**	**Other**
01:00		00:30	00:00
SS1		RS1	-
Drill Sets		Strides - Slight Downhill Course - 4-8 x 20 secs 95% effort - Proud posture, quick cadance	-

Thursday			
Resting Heart Rate:		Weight:	
Swim	**Bike**	**Run**	**Other**
00:00	00:00	01:00	00:45
-	-	RE2	SM - 3*6
-	-	Extensive Endurance - Steady Zone 2 - Cadence 90 - Rolling Course	-Squat -Seated Row -Abdominal Twist -Hamstring Curl -Chest Press

Friday

Resting Heart Rate:		Weight:	
Swim	**Bike**	**Run**	**Other**
00:00	01:00	00:00	00:00
-	BM3	-	-
-	Hill Cruise Intervals - 6-12 min Intervals uphill - Zone 4-5a - 3 min recovery in Zone 1 - Rolling Course	-	-

Saturday

Resting Heart Rate:		Weight:	
Swim	**Bike**	**Run**	**Other**
00:00	00:00	00:45	00:00
-	-	RE2	-
-	-	Extensive Endurance - Steady Zone 2 - Cadence 90 - Rolling Course	-

Sunday

Resting Heart Rate:		Weight:	
Swim	**Bike**	**Run**	**Other**
00:00	01:30	01:00	00:00
-	CM1	CM1	-
-	Tempo Brick -60-90min Ride w/20k time trial -15-45min at race pace	Tempo Brick -60-90min Ride w/20k time trial -15-45min at race pace	-

TOTAL

SWIM	**BIKE**	**RUN**	**OTHER**
01:00	03:30	03:30	01:30
		TOTAL	09:30

Peak **Week 12** **WC**

Monday			
Resting Heart Rate:		Weight:	
Swim	**Bike**	**Run**	**Other**
00:00	00:00	00:00	00:45
-	-	-	SM - 3*6
-	-	-	-Squat -Seated Row -Abdominal Twist -Hamstring Curl -Chest Press

Tuesday			
Resting Heart Rate:		Weight:	
Swim	**Bike**	**Run**	**Other**
	01:00		00:00
	BS1		-
	-1 min w/up -Max Cadence for Max Time -Repeat		-

Wednesday			
Resting Heart Rate:		Weight:	
Swim	**Bike**	**Run**	**Other**
01:00		00:30	00:00
SS1		RS1	-
Open Water		Strides - Slight Downhill Course - 4-8 x 20 secs 95% effort - Proud posture, quick cadence	-

Thursday			
Resting Heart Rate:		Weight:	
Swim	**Bike**	**Run**	**Other**
00:00	00:00	00:30	00:45
-	-	RE2	SM - 3*6
-	-	Extensive Endurance - Steady Zone 2 - Cadence 90 - Rolling Course	-Squat -Seated Row -Abdominal Twist -Hamstring Curl -Chest Press

Friday			
Resting Heart Rate:		Weight:	
Swim	**Bike**	**Run**	**Other**
00:00	01:00	00:00	00:00
-	BM3	-	-
-	Hill Cruise Intervals - 6-12 min Intervals uphill - Zone 4-5a - 3 min recovery in Zone 1 - Rolling Course	-	-

Saturday			
Resting Heart Rate:		Weight:	
Swim	**Bike**	**Run**	**Other**
00:00	00:00	01:00	00:00
-	-	RE2	-
-	-	Extensive Endurance - Steady Zone 2 - Cadence 90 - Rolling Course	-

Sunday			
Resting Heart Rate:		Weight:	
Swim	**Bike**	**Run**	**Other**
00:00	01:00	00:00	00:00
-	BE2	-	-
-	Extensive Endurance -Steady Zone 2 -Comfortable high cadence -Rolling Course	-	-

TOTAL			

SWIM	BIKE	RUN	OTHER
01:00	03:00	02:00	01:30
		TOTAL	07:30

Race   **Week 13**   <u>WC</u>

Monday			
Resting Heart Rate:		Weight:	
Swim	**Bike**	**Run**	**Other**
00:00	00:30	00:00	00:00
-	BE1	-	-
-	Recovery -Steady Zone 1 -Comfortable high cadence -Flat Course	-	-

Tuesday			
Resting Heart Rate:		Weight:	
Swim	**Bike**	**Run**	**Other**
	01:00		00:00
	BS3		-
	Jumps - 3-8 sec max sprints - Within Endurance Ride - RPE Zone 5c - 2 mins recovery		-

Wednesday			
Resting Heart Rate:		Weight:	
Swim	**Bike**	**Run**	**Other**
01:00		00:30	00:00
SS1		RP1	-
Open Water		Sprints - 4-8 x 20-30 sec max effort sprints - RPE Zone 5c - Quick cad, don't muscle it - 3-5 min recovery	-

Thursday			
Resting Heart Rate:		Weight:	
Swim	**Bike**	**Run**	**Other**
00:00	00:00	00:45	00:00
-	-	RS3	-
-	-	Pickups - Within Endurance Run - 20 secs intervals @ 5km pace - Several min recovery	-

Friday

Resting Heart Rate:		Weight:	
Swim	**Bike**	**Run**	**Other**
00:00	02:00	00:00	00:00
-	BE1	-	-
-	Recovery -Steady Zone 1 -Comfortable high cadence -Flat Course	-	-

Saturday

Resting Heart Rate:		Weight:	
Swim	**Bike**	**Run**	**Other**
00:00	00:30	00:15	00:00
-	CS1	CS1	-
-	Pre-Race Brick -Day Before Race -30 minute Ride -15 minute Run -3-5 accelerations within each	Pre-Race Brick -Day Before Race -30 minute Ride -15 minute Run -3-5 accelerations within each	-

Sunday

Resting Heart Rate:		Weight:	
Swim	**Bike**	**Run**	**Other**
-	-	-	-
R	A	C	E

TOTAL

SWIM	**BIKE**	**RUN**	**OTHER**
		TOTAL	

Made in the USA
Coppell, TX
29 December 2019